Picture History
of the
20th Century

THE 1920s

Richard Tames

SEA-TO-SEA
Mankato Collingwood London

This edition first published in 2006 by
Sea-to-Sea Publications
1980 Lookout Drive
North Mankato
Minnesota 56003

Printed in China

Library of Congress Cataloging-in-Publication Data

Tames, Richard.
  The 1920's / by Richard Tames.
       p. cm.—(Picture history of the 20th century)
  Originally published: New York : F. Watts, c1991.
  Includes index.
  Summary: Text and pictures highlight the main events of the 1920s.
  ISBN 1-932889-70-1
  1. Nineteen twenties—Pictorial works—Juvenile literature. [1. Nineteen twenties.] I. Title.
II. Series.

D720.T33 2005
909.82′2′0222—dc22
                                                                                          2004064982

9 8 7 6 5 4 3 2

Published by arrangement with the Watts Publishing Group Ltd, London

Photographs: The Architectural Press 43(B); Associated Press/Topham 45(BL),
45(BC); N. S. Barrett 37(T), 37(C), 37(BL); The Bettmann Archive/Hulton-Deutsch
44(BL); BFI Stills, Posters and Designs 39(T), 39(C); Martin Breese/Retrograph
Archive Collection 13(B), 33(B); Brown Brothers 21(C); Mary Evans Picture
Library 7(T), 7(C), 9(B), 10(B), 11(C), 11(B), 17(B), 19(B), 23(B), 25(B), 28(T),
29(BL); Mary Evans/Explorer 32(B); Mary Evans/Steve Rumney 32(T); Ford Motor
Archive 25(T); Robert Harding 8(BOTH); Hulton-Deutsch 12(T), 30(B), 44(BC);
The Illustrated London News 20(T); L'Illustration/Sygma 13(T), 15(B), 16(B),
18(T); Keystone/Sygma 38(B); Kobal Collection 26(BOTH), 27(ALL), 28(B), 29(T),
29(BR); Robert Opie 24(T), 43(TR); Popperfoto 6(B), 7(B), 9(T), 10(T), 11(T),
12(B), 13(C), 14(BOTH), 15(T), 16(T), 17(T), 17(C), 18(B), 23(TR), 31(C), 33(T),
37(BR); from WINNIE THE POOH by A. A. Milne, illustrated by E. H. Shephard,
copyright 1926 by E. P. Dutton, renewed 1954 by A. A. Milne, reproduced by
permission of the publisher, Dutton Children's Books, a division of Penguin Books
USA Inc. 39(b); Topham 19(T), 21(B), 44(BR), 45(BR); UPI/Bettmann 6(T), 19(C),
20(B), 21(T), 22(B), 23(TL), 24(B), 36(BOTH), 38(T), 43(BR); The Vintage
Magazine Company 22(T), 31(T), 42(BL), 43(TL); with thanks to the Visual Arts
Library 42(T); reproduced by permission of Warner Chappell Music Ltd 31(B); Val
Wilmer 30(T).

cover: Mary Evans Picture Library/Hulton-Deutsch/Kobal Collection
frontispiece: Mary Evans Picture Library

CONTENTS

Introduction

In the aftermath of World War I, neither the victors nor the vanquished had cause for celebration when the new map of Europe was drawn. Having suffered appalling wartime losses, France recovered the provinces of Alsace and Lorraine only to be haunted by the prospect of German revenge. After the costly war, British resources were drained by demobilization, the shift to a peacetime economy, and the responsibilities of an empire enlarged at Germany's expense. When Ireland finally threw off British rule, the resulting partition created more problems. Russia, shattered first by revolution and then by civil war, turned its back on Europe and transformed the remains of a tsarist empire into a socialist society. Poland and the Baltic republics were restored to independence after centuries of Russian domination. Although on the winning side, unstable Italy grew increasingly resentful over its lack of territorial gain. It spawned a new kind of political movement, Fascism, that would inspire imitation throughout the continent. When the new states of Yugoslavia and Czechoslovakia emerged, Austria and Hungary were left as independent remnants of a defeated empire, as was Turkey. A much smaller Germany, ravaged by civil disorder and inflation, bore its territorial losses and the burden of reparations with great bitterness.

Disillusioned by the European peace settlement, the United States withdrew into isolationism and refused to join the newly created League of Nations President Wilson had inspired. Americans were too absorbed in their own affairs to pay much attention to what was going on in Europe.

The nation greeted the "Roaring Twenties" with enthusiasm, dancing frenetically to the Charleston, flocking to the new talking pictures, drinking liquor in defiance of Prohibition laws, and speculating wildly in the stock market. Women shortened their skirts and bobbed their hair in celebration of their new found freedoms. With political scandals frequently making headlines, the public worshiped a new set of heroes: record-breaking sports figures, reckless stuntmen, daring airplane pilots, glamorous movie stars, and self-made millionaires.

Americans embarked on a spending spree, buying new radios, automobiles, and labor-saving appliances now that merchants had come up with the installment plan. Buyers only had to put some cash down and then they could pay off the rest, a little each month. Some authors and commentators were critical of American life and wrote at length about the excesses of materialism, but it wasn't until the stock market collapsed in 1929 that the nation knew the party was over.

The United States in the 1920s

Postwar Americans wanted a "return to normalcy" and turned away from world affairs. The government refused to join the new League of Nations and limited immigration from abroad. It also tolerated domestic repression. The Red Scare resulted in the controversial execution of anarchists Sacco and Vanzetti. In the South, the Ku Klux Klan attacked Catholics, Jews, and blacks with impunity while religious fundamentalists banned the teaching of evolution. Prohibition, the "noble experiment," made the sale and consumption of alcoholic beverages illegal nationwide. However, Americans found ways to circumvent the law, with the cooperation of corrupt politicians, police, and judges.

A rapidly expanding economy made automobiles, telephones, and radios available to millions of Americans, but in 1929, the spending spree and wild speculation came to an end with a sudden loss of confidence in the Stock Market. The economy lurched into an uncontrolled depression as businesses plunged into bankruptcy and unemployment soared. The "Roaring Twenties" ended with a whimper.

△ In 1925, John Scopes went on trial for teaching evolution in defiance of Tennessee law. The case attracted national attention when Clarence Darrow came to Scopes's defense and William Jennings Bryan testified on behalf of religious fundamentalists.

◁ The Wall Street Crash of October 24, 1929 brought a period of hectic stock market speculation to a dramatic end. Thousands of personal fortunes were lost as panic-stricken investors rushed to sell stock at any price. Those who had borrowed to speculate were forced to sell whatever they could to raise cash.

◁ President Warren G. Harding died in office before the corruption of his administration was revealed. Calvin Coolidge (below) handed the reins of government to Herbert Hoover (far left) just as the economy peaked.

◁ Victims of a Chicago gang war machine-gunned against the wall of a garage in the "St. Valentine's Day" Massacre of 1929. Prohibition of alcohol sales from 1920 onwards led to a vast illegal "booze" industry involving smuggling, extortion and shoot-outs between rival mobsters.

A New International Order

World War I began as a punitive expedition to save small nations such as Serbia and Belgium from the aggression of Germany and its allies. It ended as a crusade to "make the world safe for democracy" and to end war itself.

The peacemakers who gathered in Paris in 1919 set themselves two contradictory aims – to create a secure framework for a new international order and to humiliate and punish the defeated powers. High hopes were pinned on the newly established League of Nations, but it was gravely weakened from the outset by the refusal of the United States to join. Attempts to make Germany "pay" for war damage through massive reparations only succeeded in disrupting the recovery of the postwar European economy and were finally abandoned in 1932.

Significant but unspectacular progress was made, however, in important aspects of international cooperation such as the collection of statistics, the treatment of refugees, and promotion of labor rights. The inauguration of regular airline services between nations helped to bring them closer together but also raised fears of air warfare.

How The War – And Four Peace Treaties Changed The Map Of Europe

- Lost by Germany 1919
- Saar: League of Nations control
- Austria-Hungary until 1918
- Former territory of Imperial Russia

△ World War I destroyed three multinational empires – Russian, Ottoman and Austro-Hungarian. Successor states were troubled by minority problems.

◁ Palace of hope – the League of Nations building at Geneva in Switzerland. The League failed to end international conflicts but did much valuable work nonetheless.

▷ The Pact of Paris was signed by 15 nations in 1928 and eventually ratified by a total of 62. The signatories pledged to renounce war as a means of settling disputes but provided no means of punishing lapses or preventing undeclared wars.

▽ Each newly independent nation advertized its sovereignty by issuing its own stamps and coins and adopting a national anthem and flag. Fierce national pride and the right to erect tariff barriers made the prospects for international cooperation less hopeful.

▽ The Washington Disarmament Conference of 1921–22 scaled down the strength of the world's major navies; required the United States, France, Britain, and Japan to respect each other's Pacific possessions; and outlawed the use of gas in warfare. The 1927 Geneva Conference failed to cut navies still further.

Lenin's Russia

By mid-1920, the hastily-created Red Army had ensured the victory of the Bolsheviks over the "Whites," a loose coalition of anti-Communists supported by Western governments. A brief but bloody war with newly independent Poland was followed by widespread famine, bringing the economy to the verge of collapse. Against this gloomy background, a Union of Soviet Socialist Republics was finally established in 1922. Meanwhile, a "New Economic Policy" was swiftly introduced to reverse earlier attempts at wholesale nationalization and overcome a complete collapse in production and food supplies.

Lenin's death was then followed by a power struggle in which Stalin overcame Trotsky to emerge by 1929 as a supreme dictator, pledged to the building of "socialism in one country" rather than fomenting worldwide revolution as Trotsky had wished. This was to be done through enforced industrialization and the collectivization of agriculture and by mass terror if necessary.

△ Leon Trotsky was the creator of the Red Army which gave the Bolsheviks victory in the civil war. (Note he is wearing a uniform.) Although he was Lenin's chief lieutenant, he was eventually forced into exile in 1929 and killed on Stalin's orders in 1940.

◁ In 1920, Poland tried to take the Ukraine. Here, the Poznan Regiment waits to attack Kiev, which fell on May 7. Counterattacks took the Russians to the edge of Warsaw, where French support helped the Poles drive them back. The 1921 Treaty of Riga redefined frontiers.

△ Nikolai Bukharin, seen here addressing a Moscow crowd in 1922, never held a top political post but had great influence as editor of the party newspaper *Pravda (Truth).* He was denounced in 1928 and finally executed after a "show-trial" in 1938.

▷ The cumulative effects of war followed by a civil war led to a disastrous famine in the Volga region in 1922.

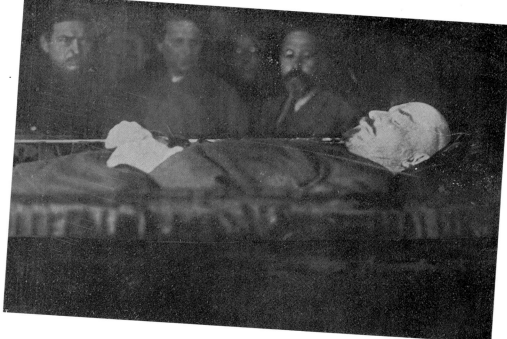

▷ Lenin, lying in state after his death in 1924. His belief that "there is room for other parties only in jail" gave a monopoly of power to the Communists but failed to secure a smooth succession to his personal control over it. In an atheist country, his mausoleum became a focus for personal pilgrimage and collective rituals.

Mussolini's Italy

Italy came out of World War I on the winning side but her meager territorial gains seemed to many patriots a poor reward for her sacrifices. Economic dislocation threatened social revolution and favored political extremism. In 1919, ex-socialist Benito Mussolini launched his *Fascio di Combattimento*, an antisocialist militia inspired by ultranationalism and with a disposition to violence. His muddled program of reform at least promised decisive action and attracted many ex-soldiers to the ranks of the Fascists. Having bluffed and bullied his way to power, Mussolini proceeded to eliminate opposition to his rule and suppress civil liberties. Parliamentary debate was replaced by parades and slogans; "Mussolini is always right," proclaimed one. Another simply required, "Believe, Obey, Fight."

▽ Ex-newspaperman Mussolini after seizing control of Rome in a bloodless coup on October 29, 1922.

△ Cyclists wearing the cockerel-feather helmets of crack Italian mountain troops hail their country's leader, "Il Duce."

◁ Mussolini rides in a procession to celebrate the tenth anniversary of his seizure of power. Jack-booted Fascists give the party's raised-arm salute. The ruins of the Roman Coliseum serve as a reminder of the past glories Mussolini sought to revive – or at least to exploit. In practice, Italy's military power was limited by its economic backwardness.

△ Pope Pius XI at his desk in the Vatican. In 1929, Mussolini achieved a major diplomatic success with the signing of the Lateran Treaty by which Italy recognized the independence of the Vatican state and accepted Roman Catholicism as the sole official religion of the country.

◁ A special postage stamp celebrates an exhibition held in Alto Adige, a northern province acquired after World War I. The local German-speaking minority resented incorporation in the Italian state. Note the "fasces," the bundle of rods, symbolizing unity, from which Fascism took its name.

Weimar Germany

On November 11, 1918, Germany accepted Allied terms for an armistice, and the Kaiser, the "supreme warlord," fled into exile in neutral Holland. With her army reeling under the hammer-blows of coordinated attacks by the advancing Allies, her navy in a state of open mutiny and her civilian population on the edge of starvation or revolt, Germany had nothing left to fight with, yet alone fight for.

Yet, when she sued for peace, no Allied army had invaded her territory. Thus was born the legend of the "dolchstoss," the "stab in the back," which alleged that Germany had never been defeated, only betrayed. And the betrayers were identified as the liberals and socialists who had signed the armistice and established a new republic based on a constitution drawn up in the elegant town of Weimar. For many Germans, the regime of the "November criminals" could command no loyalty.

Five years of political turmoil preceded an unsteady economic recovery and were accompanied by a flowering of avant-garde art, music, and drama, which seemed to traditional patriots clear proof of the degeneration of the times. The onset of depression after 1929 sealed the fate of an unloved regime.

△ Dr. Walther Rathenau, who served as minister of reconstruction and foreign minister before being assassinated by right-wing extremists after engineering the Russo-German Treaty of Rapallo which developed cooperation between the Soviet Union and Weimar Germany.

◁ French troops in the Ruhr in 1923. The presence of foreign forces on German soil proved to angry patriots the weakness of the Weimar regime. In the end, German reparation payments were to be scaled down by international agreement.

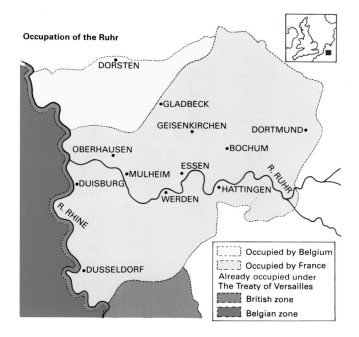

Occupation of the Ruhr

Occupied by Belgium
Occupied by France
Already occupied under
The Treaty of Versailles
British zone
Belgian zone

△ The Treaty of Versailles imposed heavy reparations payments on Germany to punish aggression and finance reconstruction. When Germany defaulted, France and Belgium sent troops into the industrial Ruhr.

▷ Adolf Hitler in prison at the fortress of Landsberg am Lech after the failure of his 1923 "beer-hall putsch." He was allowed many visitors and gained valuable publicity by writing *Mein Kampf (My Struggle)*.

◁ The strain of paying reparations undermined the German currency from 1922 onward. Here, 8,000 deutsche marks are seen as the equivalent of one dollar. The occupation of the Ruhr in 1923 led the local population to respond with passive resistance which hampered the invaders but also damaged the economy, leading to a final collapse of the currency. A new "rentenmark," introduced in November 1923, could be exchanged for one trillion old marks. The currency collapse wiped out the savings of the middle classes but enabled some speculators to make fortunes.

Men of Power

The shock waves of World War I continued long after the actual fighting ended. Political instability, together with the new power of mass media to focus attention on dramatic actions and striking personalities, created situations in which a strong leader could appear to offer decisive solutions to the many problems. Lenin and Mussolini offered clear models at opposite ends of the political spectrum.

The breakup of the immense multinational Austro-Hungarian empire made Eastern Europe especially vulnerable to authoritarian regimes. In Hungary, Admiral Miklós Horthy led counterrevolutionary forces against the communist uprising of Bela Kun and ruled the country for the next 25 years. Poland, Yugoslavia, and Greece proved to be equally vulnerable while Albania saw the adventurer Ahmed Bey Zogu transform himself from president into king in 1928.

Even some democracies seemed to find security under the guidance of a single dominating individual. In newly established Czechoslovakia, Thomas Masaryk, leader of the independence movement, ruled as president from 1918 to 1935. Greece exchanged monarchy for turmoil until Prime Minister Venizelos brought some stability (1928–32).

△ Marshal Józef Pilsudski, hero of the Russo-Polish war, was head of state of newly independent Poland until 1922. Impatient with democracy, he established a military dictatorship in 1926 which lasted until his death in 1935.

◁ Reza Shah Pahlevi with his infant son in 1926. A Cossack adventurer, he seized power in Iran in 1921, proclaimed himself Shah in 1925 and, taking Atatürk as his model, attempted a rapid modernization of the state and economy.

◁ Alexander Karadjordjevic on his wedding day in 1922. Having served as Regent for his father, Peter I, from 1918 to 1921, he ruled over the kingdom of Serbs, Croats, and Slovenes during a phase of disorderly democracy before proclaiming a dictatorship and renaming the country Yugoslavia (United Slavs) in 1929.

◁ Miguel Primo de Rivera seized control of Spain with military backing in 1923, ruling as effective dictator until economic failures forced his resignation in 1930.

△ Mustafa Kemal created the modern Turkish republic out of the ruins of the Ottoman Empire. Taking the surname of "Atatürk" ("Father Turk,") he promoted Western culture enthusiastically.

Hitting the Headlines

World War I and the political convulsions that followed it not only stimulated demand for news among readers, but also led to the extension of a worldwide news-gathering network of reporters, photographers and wire services. Newspaper chains developed, spurred by the success of the Hearst and Scripps-Howard organizations. By 1927, there were 55 chains controlling 230 daily papers. Regular coverage of sports and business, plus the addition of "women's pages" and even children's features made newspapers bulkier than before.

In 1921, photographs of mysterious depressions in the snows of the Himalayas started the legend of "Big Foot," which, like the Loch Ness Monster, provided the papers with a story that would run for years. Newspapers themselves "created" news by sponsoring competitions, exhibitions, and attempts to break sporting or speed records.

Radio and the movies brought news to the public more swiftly and more dramatically than ever before, provoking newspapers into a more visual style of news presentation.

△ The British mountaineer George Mallory leading an assault on Everest, the world's highest peak. Note the absence of breathing apparatus and special protective clothing. Mallory died in the course of his third attempt. He may have reached the summit.

◁ The great Kanto earthquake of September 1923 killed some 100,000 people in Tokyo and the port of Yokohama and rendered two million homeless. Flooding, looting, and cholera followed, but the Japanese capital was swiftly rebuilt. The picture shows survivors in makeshift shacks.

▷ Franco-Spanish forces use a heliograph to communicate in the Rif Mountains of Morocco. The revolt of Abd-al-Krim against colonial rule took five years to suppress. After 20 years in detention, he escaped to live in retirement as an inspiration for the next generation of Arab nationalists.

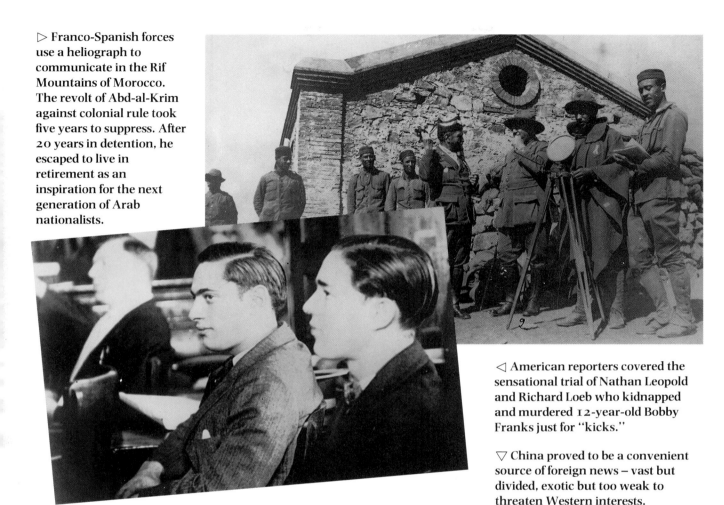

◁ American reporters covered the sensational trial of Nathan Leopold and Richard Loeb who kidnapped and murdered 12-year-old Bobby Franks just for "kicks."

▽ China proved to be a convenient source of foreign news – vast but divided, exotic but too weak to threaten Western interests.

The "Red" Menace Among the Yellow Men
THE CHINESE STRIKERS AND THEIR CITIZEN TRIBUNALS

CHINESE SERVANTS ARRESTED BY THE REDS
armed picket of the "Red" army holding up boys who attempted to reach Hong Kong, which the boycott has placed out of bounds.

WOMEN PRISONERS AND THEIR ARMED GUARDS
Two girl prisoners about to be tried by the strikers' court, an institution introduced by the Russians.

The New Woman

World War I shattered the myth of feminine frailty. Political leaders who had once denied women the vote admitted that the war could not have been won without their efforts and accepted their claim to full citizenship. In 1920, American women were permitted to cast their ballots in national elections. In 1922, Mrs. W. H. Felton of Georgia became the first woman to serve as a United States senator while in 1925, Nellie Tayloe Ross of Wyoming became the first woman governor.

Many women, having filled in for men on the home front during the war, chose to stay on in offices, shops, and factory jobs, rather than return to their prewar domestic lives. Even those who preferred to stay at home were more educated and worldly than their mothers had ever been. They felt quite sophisticated using makeup, smoking cigarettes, and acquiring a knowledge of birth control. Housewives took advantage of labor-saving devices, such as the vacuum cleaner and electric iron, and time-saving convenience foods, such as packaged breakfast cereals and quick-frozen vegetables. New magazines like *Good Housekeeping* (1922) helped them stay up-to-date with the latest trends in homemaking.

△ Amelia Earhart, the first woman to fly the Atlantic – as a passenger in 1928 and later solo in 1932. Women pilots were the supreme example of the fearless, technically capable woman.

◁ Nellie Tayloe Ross was elected to complete the remainder of her husband's term as governor of Wyoming. On the same day in 1924, "Ma" Ferguson was elected governor of Texas, but Mrs. Ross is credited as the nation's first woman governor because she took the oath of office two weeks before Mrs. Ferguson did.

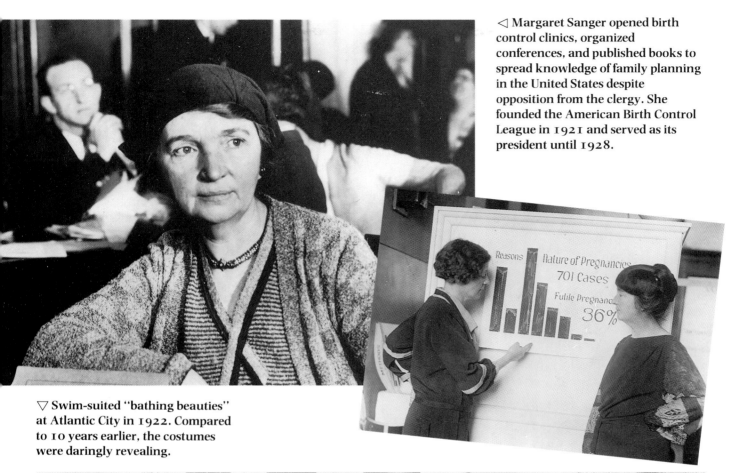

◁ Margaret Sanger opened birth control clinics, organized conferences, and published books to spread knowledge of family planning in the United States despite opposition from the clergy. She founded the American Birth Control League in 1921 and served as its president until 1928.

▽ Swim-suited "bathing beauties" at Atlantic City in 1922. Compared to 10 years earlier, the costumes were daringly revealing.

Take to the Air

At the end of World War I, many pilots were looking for work in the untested field of civil aviation. In the United States, they performed dare-devil stunts for "flying circuses" or, less romantically, flew as crop dusters for farmers. Others, like Charles Lindbergh, competed for prize money, setting records for nonstop long-distance flights. To encourage the airline industry, the government awarded contracts for airmail service to private companies. Commercial passenger service started in 1926 and only four years later, operated over routes covering almost 50,000 miles.

While civil aviation grew, military aviation declined so in 1921, Assistant Chief of the Air Service, William "Billy" Mitchell demonstrated the importance of air power by having his bombers sink three captured German warships off the Virginia coast. In 1925, after publicly criticizing his superiors, Mitchell was court-martialed. He resigned from the army in 1926, devoting the rest of his life to a crusade for an adequate air force.

In May 1926, Byrd and Bennett were the first men to fly over the North Pole. Two days later, Norwegian Amundsen's airship repeated the feat.

GREAT BRITAIN
· HOLDER ·

Nº OF WINS: 3
YEARS: 1914, 1922, 1927.

U.S.A.
Nº OF WINS: 2
YEARS: 1923, 1925.

THE JACQUES SCHNEIDER MARITIME TROPHY
Presented in 1912 to the AÉRO CLUB DE FRANCE by M. Jacques Schneider for an International Aviation Competition under Rules approved by the Federation Aeronautique Internationale

ITALY
RUNNER-UP

Nº OF WINS: 3
YEARS: 1920, 1921, 1926.

FRANCE
Nº OF WINS: 1
YEAR: 1913.

△ In 1913, the French flying enthusiast Jacques Schneider presented a trophy for an annual competition for seaplanes, consisting of an air race and seaworthiness trials. The contest boosted both public interest and technical progress in flying during the 1920s.

◁ In 1929, Lieutenant James ("Jimmy") H. Doolittle made a successful landing at Mitchell Field, New York, having piloted the first "blind" airplane, relying solely on instruments for guidance. This was an important contribution to airplane safety, making flights possible in bad weather.

△ Col. William ("Billy") Mitchell was an outspoken advocate of a separate American airforce. He claimed that the airplane made the battleship obsolete and sunk captured warships from the air to prove his point. He even anticipated the possibility of a Japanese air attack on the Hawaiian Islands.

▽ The German airship *Graf Zeppelin* entering its New Jersey hangar after crossing the Atlantic in 1924. Count (Graf) von Zeppelin built his first rigid airship in 1900 and by 1914, the airship had carried 35,000 people without accident. The 1930 crash of the British *R101* came as a severe setback to airship use.

△ On May 21, 1927, Charles Lindbergh of Minnesota became the first man to fly the Atlantic solo, non-stop. Loaded down with fuel, his *Spirit of St. Louis* lurched into the sky at Long Island to touch down 33 hours later at Le Bourget, Paris. He won $25,000 and undying fame.

The Automobile Revolution

During the 1920s, automobiles increased in popularity. Production expanded from 1.5 million cars in 1921 to 4.7 million in 1929. Chrysler was founded in 1925 to compete with Ford and General Motors. By 1926, with the invention of new finishes, automobiles could be ordered in a wide variety of colors at affordable prices. They also became more streamlined in appearance. To keep up with rapidly changing styles, Henry Ford scrapped his durable but drab Model T and introduced the snappier and very successful Model A in 1927.

The automobile changed the way most Americans lived. No longer did they have to depend on intercity trolleys or railroads to travel from place to place. Weekend trips in the family car became a national pastime. Of course, the average speed limit in the United States was only 20 miles an hour, but by the end of the decade, it moved up to 35 and 40. Businesses catering to motorists, such as filling stations, restaurants, tourist attractions, garages, and motels, sprang up along soon-to-be paved roads. Cars also freed many young couples from the restrictions of chaperones and created a more permissive atmosphere for dating.

MORRIS MINOR

THREE-SPEED TWO-SEATER
£100
ex Works

FOUR-SPEED MODELS
from £105
ex Works

△ This popular "run-about" is clearly aimed at a middle class market of golf-playing suburbanites. Like many 1920s models it was driven open or with a soft top – drafty in winter.

◁ A bad traffic accident draws a curious crowd. Poor roadmarking and streetlighting and the absence of traffic lights and driving tests meant that accident rates were high despite a low volume of traffic.

◁ The Ford Motor Company opened its first production line factory overseas at Old Trafford near Manchester before World War I. In the 1920s, it began to build a huge assembly works at Dagenham, to the east of London where the Thames gave deep-water access for ships. This new plant enabled it to meet the challenge of large-scale domestic British rivals like Morris and Austin.

▷ A French magazine illustrates the jam of motor traffic caused by spectators at an auto racing circuit. Although only the very rich could participate in auto racing, it was a sensational spectators' sport. The handbuilt racing cars of Italian Ettore Bugatti set new standards of engineering excellence which were eventually to influence the design and construction of the ordinary car.

The Movies

The movies came of age in the 1920s and Hollywood confirmed its position as the "dream factory" of the English-speaking world. It was there that fame and fortune could be found, along with movie "moguls" – producers like Cecil B. De Mille who conceived and financed pictures.

In Russia, France, and Germany, it was the directors who led the way in developing film as a serious art form. The epic *Napoleon*, directed by Frenchman Abel Gance, appeared in 1927 and is now recognized as a masterpiece of silent film technique. But in the very same year, *The Jazz Singer* broke new ground by incorporating the first live screen dialogue.

Nineteen twenty-eight saw Walt Disney's first successful sound picture, *Steamboat Willie*, featuring his most famous creation, Mickey (originally Mortimer!) Mouse. In the same year, the comedy duo of Stan Laurel and Oliver Hardy made no less than four feature films.

As movie-going became a regular weekly habit on both sides of the Atlantic, it also became a powerful vehicle for spreading American slang, dance and fashion worldwide.

△ Charlie Chaplin with Jackie Coogan in *The Kid* (1921), which Chaplin also directed. He developed a highly visual style of acting that combined a skillful use of gesture and timing with brilliant athletic skills, enabling him to contrast pathos and slapstick, moving stories forward without dialogue.

◁ The establishment of the Academy Awards showed the maturing of movies as an industry confident of its own technical and artistic standards. The name "Oscar" came from a secretary whose uncle bore a striking resemblance to the statuette so his name was given to it.

◁ The thrilling chariot race from *Ben Hur* (1926).

▽ A German poster for the Russian film *The Battleship Potemkin* (1925).

△ Sheet music for tunes from *The Jazz Singer* (1927), starring Al Jolson, a Russian immigrant whose real name was Asa Yoelson.

▷ Walt Disney with Mickey Mouse dolls in 1929. This pioneered a trend to franchising goods based on film successes.

27

The Stars

Whether or not it was their original intention, the film studios of the 1920s found that they had created "stars" whom the public would pay to see – even if the film itself did not appeal much. They remained stars just as long as they kept their popularity in a notoriously high-risk industry. It was therefore desirable that these public figures should behave accordingly. For as long as they worked obediently they were paid well, but if they showed too much independence of mind or became involved in scandal, they could find their career finished overnight – such was the fate of comedy star Roscoe "Fatty" Arbuckle.

Compliance was therefore more important than outstanding talent. Studio publicity offices enhanced the stars' earning power by feeding bits of gossip to magazines targeted at "starry-eyed" fans. Lavish homes and extravagant parties gave them a larger-than-life image which captured the hearts of film-goers on both sides of the Atlantic. Many fantasized about looking like a film star and the various imitated fashions, hair styles, and makeup showed the impact of these fantasies. The 1927 off-screen romance of on-screen lovers John Gilbert and Swedish actress Greta Garbo was another sensational example of reality imitating fantasy.

RUDOLPH VALENTINO & VILMA BANKY.
IN "THE SON OF THE SHEIK".
ALLIED ARTISTS PICTURE.   236.P.
BEAGLES' POSTCARDS
'FAMOUS CINEMA STAR' SERIES.

△ Rudolph Valentino starring in *The Son of the Sheik*, a sequel to *The Sheik* which shot him to stardom in 1922. Valentino's death in 1926 from peritonitis was followed by a showy funeral with emotional scenes from devoted fans.

◁ The star who outlasted them all. More than 50 years after his first appearance on screen, spinach-eating Popeye was still going strong. The appeal of cartoon films, with their ingenious visual humor, went beyond the boundaries of time, space, and language.

◁ Timid-looking comedian Harold Lloyd specialized in daring slapstick stunts which were sometimes as dangerous as they looked. Silent acting required many stars to develop athletic skills to make their impact.

"Buster" Keaton (below) in *Sherlock Jr.* Known as "Frozen Face," he was a master of comic timing and gesture. The ones who got away (below left). Swashbuckling Douglas Fairbanks and Mary Pickford joined with Charlie Chaplin to create "United Artists" as a new company outside of major studio control.

The Jazz Age

It was said that if you needed to ask what jazz was, you wouldn't understand the answer. Jazz allegedly spoke to the emotions, not the intellect; the feet, not the brain. It developed around the turn of the century in the South, drawing on black work songs, spirituals, and other musical forms whose harmonies and rhythms were of African and, to a lesser extent, European inspiration.

Not until the 1920s did it attract attention outside its region of birth, spreading north and west and being imitated and adapted by white musicians. Of these, the most famous was Paul Whiteman, a disillusioned classical musician whose band's first record, "Whispering/Japanese Sandman," sold two million copies. Whiteman offered his listeners well-drilled orchestration, punctuated with brief "hot" interludes, thrown in to liven the action. It might have been novel, but anyone who had actually experienced New Orleans or a Harlem nightclub knew that it wasn't jazz. The jazz of the "dives" and "speakeasies" aroused fear and fury in the self-appointed defenders of respectable society and conventional cultural standards. They denounced jazz as "primitive," an incitement to sin and an accompaniment to crime. Jazz certainly got music talked about!

△ Louis Daniel Armstrong ("Satchmo-Satchelmouth") was already billed as "the world's greatest trumpeter" by the late 1920s. Emerging in New Orleans, he transferred to Chicago after 1922 and recorded with his own band, the "Hot Five." His genius for improvisation boosted the role of the soloist.

◁ Edward Kennedy ("Duke") Ellington with the all-black big band he formed in 1918. An outstanding pianist, he also excelled as an arranger and composer of such standards as *Mood Indigo*. From 1927 to 1932, he starred at Harlem's celebrated Cotton Club.

◁ A fantasy celebration of the "big band" sound suggesting glamour, elegance, romance and the dinner-jacketed high-life of the social elite. Spectacle on this scale represented major commercial investment and therefore offered bland adaptations of the "hot" music found in fringe night clubs. Note the all-white cast.

△ British-born violinist Yehudi Menuhin, seen here at the age of 13, made his debut in San Francisco at age 7. The child prodigy went on to a long career as a performer and teacher.

◁ *Rhapsody in Blue* by George Gershwin baffled critics when it crossed the bounds of color and tradition to blend jazz with the classical approach.

Dance, Dance, Dance

Some saw the scale of the dance craze of the 1920s as an unconscious affirmation of life and gaiety against the gruesome and haunting memories of World War I. Others argued that drabness of city life and the sheer monotony of their routine jobs drew young people to the bright lights and peppy music of nightclubs, hotel ballrooms, and dance halls. Unlike the more sedate two-step their parents found daring, young people wriggled and kicked up their heels to the Charleston and the Black Bottom. They also danced in pairs to a sensuous tango or a smooth fox-trot.

Serious dance recitals also drew large audiences. Isadora Duncan, Ruth St. Denis, and Ted Shawn brought modern dance to Europe and America while classical ballerina Anna Pavlova formed her own troupe and toured the major cities of the world.

In 1923, a craze for dance marathons swept America. Promoters offered big money prizes and contestants danced for 40 or 50 hours, until they literally dropped.

Dance halls became the most popular places for young people to meet future marriage partners.

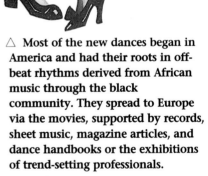

△ Most of the new dances began in America and had their roots in off-beat rhythms derived from African music through the black community. They spread to Europe via the movies, supported by records, sheet music, magazine articles, and dance handbooks or the exhibitions of trend-setting professionals.

◁ The controversial Isadora Duncan developed a style of barefoot dancing based on "natural impulses" and modeled on the inspiration of classic Greek art. Less popular in her native America than in Europe, she also founded a school in Berlin and made many visits to Russia. Her personal life was marked by open love affairs, the tragic loss of her children, and her own bizarre death.

▷ Frank Farnum, creator of the "Charleston," demonstrates the new dance with the help of one of his pupils. When it arrived in Britain, it was denounced as dangerous and provoked a newspaper campaign to ban it. Dance halls even put up notices asking their patrons to "Please Charleston Quietly."

◁ If the Charleston was intended to be outrageous fun, the sinuous, elegant tango from Argentina was equally clearly intended to be romantic. Note the high-fashion dress of the dancers, despite the fact that they are supposed to be at an afternoon tea dance, rather than at a nightclub in the early hours of the morning. The slower pace of the tango made it attractive to older dancers or as an interval item between faster numbers.

Fashion

High fashion in the 1920s was dominated by the idea of liberation. During World War I, women had taken men's jobs in factories and on farms. They soon proved, to themselves as well as others, that they could do more and earn more than men had ever thought possible. When the war ended, many discarded their uniforms and working clothes, but were eager to hang on to their new-found independence.

The Paris designer "Coco" Chanel led the way in adopting masculine fabrics such as jersey, flannel, tweed, and corduroy and introducing "practical" garments like the trench coat, sweater, and cardigan as high-fashion elements for women. On the other hand, makeup became respectable for women, other than actresses, to use in emphasizing their femininity.

The trend towards shorter skirts gave a new importance to stockings and shoes as fashion items. Rayon – known as "artificial silk" and used as a substitute for that expensive material – became available at the end of the decade and was at first almost exclusively used for stockings.

Naturally, such radical changes provoked criticism. In Italy, bishops banned bare-legged women from church. In Britain, doctors alleged short skirts caused puffy, chafed legs.

"I'm too shy to sit on your knee - but I don't mind sitting on your OXFORDS!"

▽ With the invention of the permanent wave in 1926, millions of women adapted a new hair style.

△ "Oxford Bags" originated among the wealthy students of that university.

▷ A French advertisement for swimwear. Rubber swimming caps were first of all used for the very practical purpose of protecting expensive hair styles from the water, but soon became multi-colored fashion accessories in their own right. Suntanning became a new craze among the young rich, showing that they had the leisure to do nothing in summer and go south in winter.

△ The "New Woman" of the 1920s favored the active life and adopted masculine styles for riding or driving. Note the man's soft felt hat and immaculate "spats" worn over stylish shoes. Headgear was still thought essential to complete any outfit.

▷ "I remember you when you were in long skirts," the fashionable old gentleman tells the young "flapper." Many new fashions seemed to turn established ideas upside down. Note that both of them are wearing gloves and carrying canes.

Sports

Sports became big business in the 1920s as radio outside broadcasting made it possible for anyone to "listen in" on a great event. The very predictability of sporting fixtures helped newspapers in their planning and provided a steady flow of dramatic pictures and complex records and statistics to fill their pages. Growing popular interest in sports as a spectator activity expanded the scale of each event. World heavyweight boxing champion Jack Dempsey drew crowds of over one million people between 1919 and 1926.

Nineteen twenty-three saw the opening of New York's huge Yankee Stadium and of London's Wembley Stadium which could hold 100,000 spectators. They could see not only soccer but also tennis, boxing, ice hockey, and greyhound racing, a new sport in which the lighting, totalizator, and hare all showed the growing importance of electricity.

Rewards also got bigger. In 1925, college football hero Red Grange joined the Chicago Bears – for $3,000 a game.

△ Gertrude Caroline Ederle held 29 different American and world swimming records between 1921 and 1925. In 1926 she became the first woman to swim the English channel, in 14 hours, 31 minutes.

◁ Robert Tyre ("Bobby") Jones, Jr., was a sports hero who popularized golf in the United States. He won the U.S. Open in 1923, 1926, and 1929, and the U.S. Amateur championship in 1924, 1925, 1927, and 1928.

▷ At the 1928 Olympic Games, Paavo Nurmi (center), the "Flying Finn," confirmed his status as the world's greatest middle-distance runner.

▽ "Babe Ruth" was sport's first superstar. In the 1927 season he hit 60 home runs, a record that stood for 34 years. Swimmer Johnny Weissmuller (below right), the first man to swim 100 meters under one minute, won Olympic medals before a film career as Tarzan. Scottish missionary Eric Liddell (bottom right) refused to run on a Sunday at the 1924 Paris Olympics.

Readers and Writers

In the 1920s, many writers were critical of American society. In his *The Sun Also Rises* and *A Farewell to Arms*, expatriate Ernest Hemingway voiced the disillusion of the "lost generation" whose hopes were destroyed by war. Sinclair Lewis, meanwhile, depicted the complacency and hypocrisy of small-town life in his novels *Main Street* and *Babbitt*. Willa Cather's 1922 Pulitzer Prize winning novel *One of Ours* mourned the passing of frontier values. F. Scott Fitzgerald's *This Side of Paradise* and *The Great Gatsby* described the empty lives of the wealthy.

The Harlem Renaissance produced writers such as Langston Hughes and James Weldon Johnson who expressed the bitterness of black Americans.

In Europe, T. S. Eliot took poetry in new directions while writers in the "modernism" movement, Virginia Woolf (*To the Lighthouse*), James Joyce (*Ulysses*), and Franz Kafka (*The Trial*) offered readers radical shifts of style and viewpoint.

△ Eugene O'Neill completed three Pulitzer Prize winning plays during the 1920s: *Beyond the Horizon*, *Anna Christie*, and *Strange Interlude*. His dramas examined the lives of social outcasts such as drug addicts and derelicts.

◁ Adolf Hitler's *Mein Kampf (My Struggle)* was written during his imprisonment after the failure of his attempted Munich Putsch. A rambling mixture of self-justifying autobiography, cynical political analysis and anti-Semitic propaganda, it was destined to cast a long shadow over the next 20 years of world history.

▷ More than 50 years after they were published, two of the decade's major novels were turned into full-length feature films – F. Scott Fitzgerald's *The Great Gatsby*, a critique of a world of glittering emptiness, and E. M. Forster's *A Passage to India* (below), a study of friendship and racial tension.

▽ Christopher Robin puts Eeyores's tail back in place while Winnie the Pooh looks on encouragingly. A. A. Milne's immortal characters continued to delight each generation of children for the rest of the century.

Science and Medicine

The great medical advance of the decade came in 1928 with Alexander Fleming's discovery of penicillin – the first major antibiotic. It was to take 15 years, however, before a practical method of large-scale manufacture was to be developed at Oxford by the Australian pathologist Howard Florey and his team. A more immediate result was seen with the isolation of the hormone insulin by the Canadians Banting and Best in 1921. This helped to revolutionize the treatment of diabetes.

Nineteen twenty-two also saw the award of the Nobel Prize for Chemistry to the Dane Niels Bohr for his research into the structure of the atom. But, again, the full significance of his work was not to be appreciated for many years. Einstein's theory of relativity had won him the Nobel Prize for Physics in 1921. Although few could understand its importance outside the scientific community, both the man and his work did catch the public imagination.

△ The introduction of dial telephones, pioneered in Chicago, reduced the average time for connecting calls from 62 seconds to 27.

▷ In 1923, archaeologist Howard Carter uncovered the tomb of 18th dynasty Egyptian pharaoh Tutankhamen. Public interest in archaeology was stimulated both by the scale and splendor of the finds and the sensational news coverage of the sudden death of Carter's patron, the Earl of Carnarvon. "Curse of the Pharaohs" screamed the headlines.

△ (Sir) Alexander Fleming, discoverer of penicillin, seen here at his workbench in St. Mary's Hospital, London. (Inset) A massively enlarged image of *Penicillium notatum*. It was Fleming's second major discovery.

▷ John Logie Baird gave the world's first public demonstration of television in Soho, London, on January 26, 1926, transmitting the image of a ventriloquist's dummy. Baird was one of the last of the great inventors, trying to turn a brilliant hunch into practical technology. Although hailed as "the father of television," Baird was to be bitterly disappointed when his system was dropped a decade later. Television still remained a curiosity in the 1920s but in 1928, the first regularly scheduled television programs were shown in Schenectady, New York.

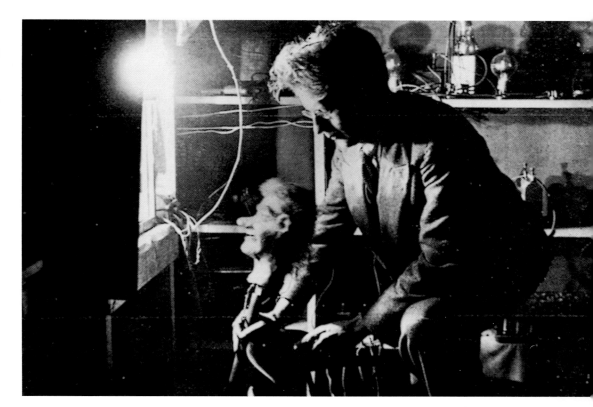

Art and Design

Design increasingly distinguished itself from art in the course of the decade. In 1919, the celebrated "Bauhaus" design school opened in Germany with architect Walter Gropius as its first director.

Nineteen twenty saw the first publication of the avant-garde magazine *L'Esprit Nouveau (The New Spirit)* founded by the Swiss-French architect Le Corbusier. In 1928 came *Domus*, an Italian journal devoted to design. In the same year, France set up the École de la Chambre Syndicale de la Couture.

Advances in new technology and research methods also opened up new possibilities. In 1926, the American chemicals giant Du Pont launched a wide range of synthetic paint colors. In the same year, the Berlei company produced a range of underwear based on a scientific analysis of body types.

▽ **Folding draft screens – a blend of modern and traditional design.**

▷ **A poster for the influential Bauhaus design school by Paul Klee.**

▽ **When Clarence Birdseye invented frozen foods in 1929, homemakers wanted refrigerators with freezers.**

28   ‖‖‖‖‖‖‖‖‖‖‖‖‖‖‖‖‖‖‖‖‖‖‖‖ MY LADY'S HOME ‖‖‖‖‖‖‖‖‖‖‖‖‖‖‖‖‖‖‖‖‖‖‖‖‖‖‖

Four-fold Draught Screens—covered in Canvas of various shade

Browns, Blues, Black, Grey, Wine colour, Red, etc.   Height 5 ft. 8 in.
These delightful Screens are decorated in various ways.

No. 281/29.
Tops mounted with the charming "Old London Cries" prints.
Price .. **£4 14 6**

No. 282/29.
Mounted with copies of "Morland" pictures.
Price .. **£4 14 6**

Decorated with
Pri

11335

Mahogany Colour and Carved Gilt Table Standard, wired 3 yds. flexible wire and key switch holder complete.

Price - £3 15 0

Cretonne and Silk Shade 12 in. dia.

Price - £1 10 0

WARING & GILLOW LTD.
OXFORD STREET. W. I.

◁ As more homes acquired electricity, demand for new appliances rose. In 1926, the pop-up toaster first appeared.

△ The Paris Exhibition of 1925 proved to be the major artistic event of the decade popularizing "art decoratif" – the style now known as "art deco."

◁ The German Pavilion for the 1929 International Exhibition at Barcelona was a triumphant example of the style of the German-American architect Mies van der Rohe. A small one-story building, it nevertheless demonstrated the basic elements he was to employ repeatedly – the use of richly colored or textured materials, bold vertical and horizontal surfaces at right angles, transparent external walls and the use of load-bearing columns, freeing partitions to be disposed of at will. To furnish the Pavilion, Mies designed an equally distinctive chair, stool and glass-topped table.

Personalities of the 1920s

Armstrong, Louis Daniel ("Satchmo") (1900–71), black American jazz musician known for his solo improvisations on the trumpet.

Bow, Clara (1905–65), American star of the silent screen whose appearance in *It* (1927) advertised a sex appeal that made her known as the "It Girl."

Bryan, William Jennings (1860–1925), American political leader and advocate of fundamentalism, who appeared for the prosecution in the Scopes trial, contesting Tennessee law banning the teaching of evolution in schools.

Bukharin, Nikolai (1888–1938), Russian co-author of the *ABC of Communism* and a member of the Politburo (1924–29) who fell from power after opposing the collectivization of agriculture and was executed in 1938.

Byrd, Richard (1888–1957), American naval aviator and explorer who flew over the North Pole in 1926. He also flew the Atlantic from west to east in 1927 and in 1929 flew over the South Pole.

Carter, Howard (1873–1939), English archaeologist in Egypt who uncovered the tomb of the Pharaoh Tutankhamen in 1922 and spent the next 10 years removing and recording its treasures.

Chaplin, Charlie (1889–1977), the world's first superstar as a result of such films as *The Kid* (1921).

Coolidge, Calvin (1872–1933), 30th president of the United States.

Coward, (Sir) Noel (1899–1973), began acting at the age of 12 and achieved notoriety as a playwright. His *Bitter Sweet* (1929) became an enduring success and confirmed his status as the most versatile theatrical talent of his day.

Darrow, Clarence Seward (1857–1938), American lawyer, famous for representing the underdog, who defended John Scopes's right to teach evolution in Tennessee.

De Mille, Cecil B. (1881–1959), American film director noted for his Biblical spectaculars and epics which used casts of thousands. He made *The Ten Commandments* and *King of Kings*, among others.

Dempsey, Jack (1895–1983), American world heavyweight boxing champion known as the "Manassa Mauler."

Eisenstein, Sergei Mikhailovich (1898–1948), Russian film director who chronicled the achievements of the Russian revolution while pioneering new cinematic techniques such as montage (editing and assembling pieces of film) and the "super close-up" in *The Battleship Potemkin* (1925) and *October* (1927).

Eliot, Thomas Stearns (1888–1965), American-born Oxford philosophy student who turned to poetry and supported himself by working in a bank. His unhappy marriage drove him to the edge of a breakdown but did not prevent him from completing *The Waste Land*, which brought him fame in 1922. In 1927 he became a British subject and joined the Church of England.

Fairbanks, Douglas (1883–1939), American film star (born Julius Ullman) who starred in *The Mark of Zorro* (1920), *The Thief of Baghdad* (1924) and *The Black Pirate* (1926).

Fitzgerald, Francis Scott (1896–1940), regarded as literary spokesman of the "Jazz Age," celebrating life in the 1920s in his novels *This Side of Paradise* (1920), *The Beautiful and the Damned* (1921), and *The Great Gatsby* (1922).

Gershwin, George (1898–1937), American songwriter and composer who combined traditional and jazz styles in his longer works *Rhapsody in Blue* (1924) and *An American in Paris* (1928).

Harding, Warren Gamaliel (1865–1923), Republican, 29th president of the United States.

Louis Armstrong

T. S. Eliot

Warren Harding

Hemingway, Ernest (1899–1961), emerged as representative of the "lost generation" of Paris-based American expatriates with the publication of his novels *The Sun Also Rises* (1926) and *A Farewell to Arms* (1929).

Hindenburg, Paul von (1847–1934), despite his advanced age, won spectacular victories during World War I to become a Field Marshal and national hero. He was elected president (1925) and served as a much-needed symbol of stability and continuity.

Hitler, Adolf (1889–1945), as a disillusioned ex-soldier, Hitler was drawn into fringe politics, joining the German Workers Party which he transformed into the National Socialist (Nazi) party. An abortive coup attempt cost him a prison sentence but made him a national figure and helped place his party at the forefront of challenge to the shaky Weimar regime.

Hoover, Herbert Clark (1874–1964), republican, 31st president of the United States.

Houdini, Harry (1874–1926), Hungarian-born Ehrich Weiss renamed himself after a French magician, became an American citizen and won fame as a spectacular escapologist and exposer of fake mediums.

Le Corbusier, Charles Édouard Jeanneret (1887–1965), Swiss-French architect who applied industrial forms to housing. In 1923, he published *Towards a New Architecture* to popularize his views.

Lenin, Vladimir Ilyich (1870–1924), creator of the Soviet Union and also of the Bolshevik party, which served many revolutionary movements as a model of disciplined action.

Lewis, (Harry) Sinclair (1885–1951), American novelist who achieved fame with satires on the small town life of the American midwest (*Main Street* [1920], *Babbitt* [1922]) and became the first American to win the Nobel Prize for Literature in 1930.

Mallory, George Leigh (1886–1924), led the first attempt on Mount Everest in 1921 and reached a record height the following year before being forced back by bad weather. He died on his third attempt, having been last seen alive a mere 800 feet below the summit.

Mussolini, Benito (1883–1945), creator of Fascist Italy whose regime served as a model for would-be right-wing revolutionaries throughout Europe.

Pickford, Mary (1893–1979), Canadian-born Gladys Smith who became "America's Sweetheart" in films like *Tess of the Storm Country* (1922).

Sanger, Margaret Higgins (1883–1966), trained as a nurse and became a fervent promoter of birth control, organizing the first American conference on family planning in 1923, and arrested many times for her activities.

Shaw, George Bernard (1856–1950), Irish dramatist and social critic whose stature was confirmed by *St. Joan* (1924) and the award of the Nobel Prize for Literature in 1925. He gave away the prize money. In 1928, he published *The Intelligent Woman's Guide to Socialism and Capitalism*.

Stresemann, Gustav (1878–1929), German statesman who, as chancellor (1923) and foreign minister (1923–9), struggled to establish his defeated country as a respected but cooperative European power. In 1926, he shared the Nobel Peace Prize with French statesman Aristide Briand (1862–1932).

Trotsky, Leon (1879–1940), Russian revolutionary, born Lev Davidovich Bronstein, who took the name of one of his jailers after escaping from Siberian exile. An advocate of world revolution, he was expelled from the party in 1927.

Paul von Hindenburg

Herbert Hoover

Gustav Stresemann

1920s Year by Year

1920

- Establishment of the League of Nations.
- Prohibition introduced in the United States.
- Nazi party established.
- Reza Khan seizes power in Iran.
- Treaty of Trianon dismembers the former Austro-Hungarian empire.
- Seventh Olympic games held at Antwerp.
- Russo-Polish war.
- Joan of Arc canonized as a saint.
- Nicola Sacco and Bartolomeo Vanzetti arrested for the murder of two men in a Massachusetts shoe factory.
- Nineteenth Amendment to the United States Constitution gives women the right to vote in federal elections.
- Treaty of Sèvres dismembers the former Ottoman Empire.
- Bolsheviks defeat "Whites" and their Western supporters in Russia.
- Warren G. Harding elected president of the United States.
- Woodrow Wilson, outgoing American president, wins Nobel Peace Prize.
- First radio stations opened in the United States (KDKA, Pittsburgh) and Britain (Chelmsford).
- First airmail flight from New York to San Francisco.

1921

- First flight by a helicopter.
- Quota Act limits immigration to the United States.
- Sun Yat-sen elected president of China.
- Communist party established in China.
- Mongolia declares itself independent as the world's second communist state.
- Unemployment in the United States reaches 5.7 million.

- Kingdom of Iraq established.
- Albert Einstein wins Nobel Prize for Physics.
- United States, Britain, Japan, and France sign Washington Treaty limiting naval armaments in the Pacific region.
- Insulin discovered as a treatment for diabetes.
- Johnson and Johnson introduce "Band-aid," the first stick-on bandage.

1922

- Pius XI succeeds Benedict XV as pope.
- Egypt proclaimed formally independent of Britain.
- First edition of *Reader's Digest* published.
- Hermann Rorschach introduces his famous inkblot test.
- Mrs. W. H. Felton becomes first woman to serve as U.S. senator.
- Fascist "March on Rome" puts Mussolini into power.
- Mustafa Kemal proclaims Turkey a republic with himself as president.
- Eugene O'Neill's *Anna Christie* wins Pulitzer Prize for drama.

1923

- Aeroflot, the national airline of the Soviet Union, is founded.
- Mussolini dissolves all opposition parties in Italy.
- Earthquake destroys much of Tokyo and Yokohama.
- President Warren Harding dies in office and is succeeded by Calvin Coolidge.
- Lee de Forest demonstrates process for motion pictures with sound.
- Miguel Primo de Rivera leads army coup in Spain.
- Collapse of German currency.
- Hitler arrested after failure of a putsch in Munich.

- French and Belgian troops occupy the Ruhr.
- Patent issued for Colonel Jacob Schick for the first electric razor.
- Bulldozer is invented.
- Paavo Nurmi runs the mile in 4 minutes, 10.4 seconds.
- Teapot Dome Scandal investigations begin in Washington, D.C.

1924

- Death of Lenin – Petrograd renamed Leningrad in his honor.
- First Winter Olympics held at Chamonix, France.
- Death of Woodrow Wilson.
- First execution by gas chamber in the United States.
- Ford Motor Company produces 10 millionth automobile.
- Italy annexes free city of Fiume.
- U.S. Congress limits Japanese immigration.
- Metro-Goldwyn Mayer film corporation established.
- Assassination of Italian socialist leader Giacomo Matteotti.
- Dawes Plan agreed for German war reparations.
- Ibn Saud captures Mecca.
- Kimberley Clark introduces first disposable handkerchiefs – Celluwipes, later known as Kleenex.
- United States grants full citizenship to native American Indians.
- Calvin Coolidge elected president of the United States.

1925

- Mussolini assumes full dictatorial powers.
- The Chrysler Corporation founded by Walter P. Chrysler.
- Chiang Kai-shek succeeds Sun Yat-sen as leader of the Chinese Nationalist Party (Kuomintang).
- Scopes trial attracts national

attention testing a Tennessee law banning the teaching of evolution in schools.
- Kurdish uprising suppressed in Turkey.
- Field Marshal von Hindenburg elected president of Germany.
- Exposition des Arts Décoratifs in Paris.
- American air power advocate Colonel William ("Billy") Mitchell is court-martialed and found guilty of insubordination.
- Hitler's *Mein Kampf (My Struggle)* published.
- Locarno Treaty reaffirms the post-war European settlement.
- G. B. Shaw wins Nobel Prize for Literature and gives away the prize money.
- First "motel" opened in California.
- Wyoming's Nellie Tayloe Ross becomes first woman governor in the United States.

1926

- Lufthansa airline founded in Germany.
- RCA organizes the National Broadcasting Company, the first nationwide radio network.
- Safeways chain of general stores established in Maryland.
- Hindu-Muslim riots in India.
- Soviet-German friendship treaty.
- Robert H. Goddard fires first liquid fuel rocket.
- The U.S. Congress creates the Army Air Corps.
- Abd-al-Krim revolt in Morocco crushed.
- American Gertrude Ederle becomes the first woman to swim the English channel.
- Hirohito becomes Emperor of Japan in his own right.
- Mussolini bans women from public offices and taxes bachelors.
- Book of the Month Club founded.
- Anti-freeze for car radiators allows all-year motoring.
- Zipper replaces buttons on jeans.
- Ernest Hemingway's *The Sun Also Rises* published.
- Floyd Bennett and Richard Byrd fly over the North Pole.
- First pop-up toaster invented in the United States.

1927

- The Holland Tunnel opens, linking New York and New Jersey.
- American Charles A. Lindbergh flies nonstop from New York to Paris in 33.5 hours.
- Major Segrave sets new world land-speed record.
- Chiang Kai-shek captures Shanghai.
- Jerome Kern and Oscar Hammerstein II's *Showboat* opens in New York.
- Ahmed Sukarno founds the Indonesian Nationalist Party.
- Harlem Globetrotters basketball team forms.
- First "talking picture," *The Jazz Singer*, exhibited.
- Stalin expels Trotsky and Zinoviev from the Soviet Communist party.
- Babe Ruth hits 60 home runs for the New York Yankees.
- Wall-mounted can opener introduced.
- First Volvo car manufactured.
- Prototype iron lung incorporates parts from two old vacuum cleaners.

1928

- Britain gives women over 21 the vote.
- Walt Disney releases first animated film to use sound.
- The Pact of Paris outlaws war.
- Amelia Earhart becomes the first woman to fly the Atlantic.
- Ninth Olympic Games held in Amsterdam.
- Fleming discovers penicillin.
- Chiang Kai-shek proclaimed president of China.
- Stalin issues Five-Year Plan for economic development in the Soviet Union.
- Eruption of Mount Etna.
- Herbert Hoover elected as president of the United States.
- Geiger counter invented.
- "Rice Krispies" introduced.
- First scheduled television broadcasts in Schenectady, New York.
- George Gershwin composes *An American in Paris.*
- "Scotch tape" goes on sale in America.

1929

- King Alexander I becomes dictator of Yugoslavia.
- U.S. Army plane flies 150 hours nonstop.
- St. Valentine's Day massacre of six Chicago gangsters.
- Mussolini signs Lateran Treaty establishing the Vatican state.
- "Oscar" awards established.
- Museum of Modern Art opens in New York.
- Stephen Vincent Benét's poem *John Brown's Body* wins Pulitzer Prize.
- German airship *Graf Zeppelin* flies around the world in 20 days, 4 hours, 14 minutes.
- Popular radio shows "Amos 'n' Andy" premieres.
- Clarence Birdseye markets frozen foods.
- Wall Street crashes as New York Stock Exchange prices plunge.
- Kodak introduces 16mm color movie film.
- U.S. aviator Richard Byrd flies over the South Pole.
- Kitchen waste disposer introduced.
- Foam rubber produced.

Index